D0492643

Religions Around the World

Judaism

Anita Ganeri

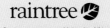

raintree

a Capstone company — publishers for children

1

Raintree is an imprint of Capstone Global Library Limited, a company incorporated in England and Wales having its registered office at 264 Banbury Road, Oxford, OX2 7DY – Registered company number: 6695582

www.raintree.co.uk
myorders@raintree.co.uk

Edited by Linda Staniford
Designed by Jenny Bergstrom
Picture research by Pam Mitsakos
Production by Steve Walker
Originated by Capstone Global Library
Printed and bound in China

ISBN 978 1 4747 4216 0
21 20 19 18 17
10 9 8 7 6 5 4 3 2 1

British Library Cataloguing in Publication Data
A full catalogue record for this book is available from the British Library.

Acknowledgements
We would like to thank the following for permission to reproduce photographs:
Alamy: Agencja Fotograficzna Caro, 7, ASAP, 21, Ira Berger, 18, PhotoStock-Israel, 22, PS-I, 16; Bridgeman Images: Archives Charmet, 9; Dreamstime: © Rafael Ben-ari, 29; Getty Images: Burke/Triolo Productions, 24, Dorling Kindersley, 8, Randy Risling, 17; iStockphoto: efesenko, 12, tovfla, 27; Newscom: CHUCK BERMAN/KRT, 19, P Deliss /GODONG/picture-alliance, 20, Rafael Ben-Ari/Chameleons Eye, 6; Shutterstock: alefbet, 28, artmig, 10, AVA Bitter, cover middle, 1 middle, blueeyes, 11, ChameleonsEye, 26, Donna Ellen Coleman, 23, eFesenko, 14, 15, karen roach, design element, Kletr, 25, Rostislav Ageev, 4, Sean Pavone, 5, ungvar, 13

We would like to thank Reverend Laurence Hillel of the London Inter Faith Centre for his invaluable help in the preparation of this book.

Every effort has been made to contact copyright holders of material reproduced in this book. Any omissions will be rectified in subsequent printings if notice is given to the publisher.

All the internet addresses (URLs) given in this book were valid at the time of going to press. However, due to the dynamic nature of the internet, some addresses may have changed, or sites may have changed or ceased to exist since publication. While the author and publisher regret any inconvenience this may cause readers, no responsibility for any such changes can be accepted by either the author or the publisher.

Contents

Some words are shown in bold, **like this.**
You can find out what they mean by
looking in the glossary.

What is Judaism?

Judaism is a religion that began in the **Middle East.** It began more than 3,500 years ago. Today, more than 14 million people follow Judaism.

The Western Wall in Jerusalem is the last remaining part of the Temple. It is a very **holy** place for Jews.

The Star of David is on the national flag of Israel.
It is the symbol of the Jewish people.

People who follow Judaism are called Jews. Jews live all over the world. Israel is the country with the most Jews. Around 290,000 Jews live in Britain.

Jewish beliefs

Jews believe in one God who created the universe and everything in it. They believe that God made a special agreement, called God's Covenant, with the Jews. God promised to look after the Jews. In return, the Jews promised to obey God.

Jews fix a case called a mezuzah on the doors of their homes. Inside are the words of a Jewish prayer.

Being part of a family and part of the Jewish community is very important to Jews.

The Jews believe that God chose them to set an example of **holiness** in the world. They try to live their lives in a good and **holy** way. This is how they keep their promise to God.

Abraham and Sarah travelled the land, telling people about the God they worshipped.

The story of Judaism began thousands of years ago. At that time, people worshipped many gods. A man named Abraham began to worship one God. Abraham is called the father of the Jews.

Moses was another important Jewish leader. At that time, the Jews lived in Egypt as slaves. But the **pharaoh** wanted to kill them. Moses led the Jews out of Egypt. Later, they reached safety in Canaan (modern-day Israel). This journey is called the **Exodus**.

In the story of the Exodus, God parted the waters of the Red Sea so that Moses could lead the Jews to safety.

9

Holy books

The **holy** book for Jews is called the Torah. Jews believe that God spoke the Torah to Moses on Mount Sinai in Egypt and that Moses then wrote it down. The Torah is made up of five books.

Jews believe Moses received the Ten Commandments, which are part of the Torah, on two stone tablets.

The Torah tells the story of how the Jews came to know about God's teaching. It also sets out the rules that guide Jews about how to live. The best-known teachings are called the **Ten Commandments.**

The Torah is written on **scrolls** in **Hebrew**.

The Torah **scrolls** are very precious. In the **synagogue,** they are wrapped in velvet covers. They are kept in a special cupboard called the **Holy** Ark.

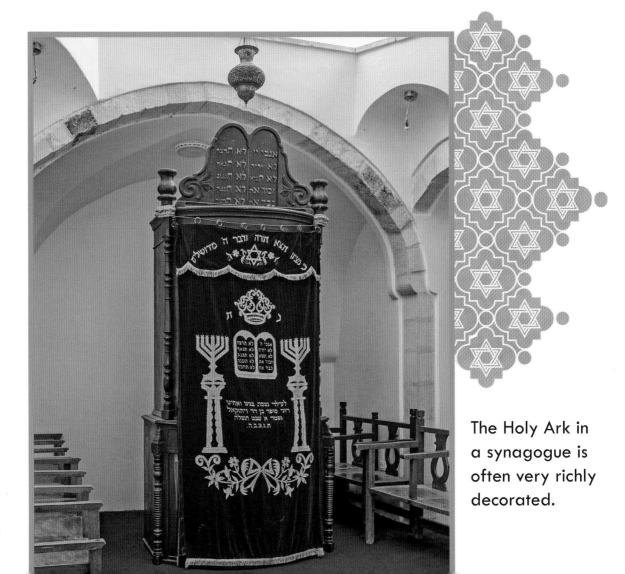

The Holy Ark in a synagogue is often very richly decorated.

The Torah scrolls are read using a special pointer called a yad.

During services, the scrolls are taken out of the Ark to be read. They are carried around the synagogue while people sing prayers. Then they are placed on a reading desk in front of the Ark.

Jewish worship

A **synagogue** is a place where Jews go to worship God. It is also a place to meet friends and where children can learn more about their religion.

This very old synagogue in Jerusalem has beautiful wall paintings.

14

The light above
the Ark is called
the Ner Tamid.

The **Holy** Ark is at the front of
the synagogue. A light always
burns above it as a sign of God's
presence. People face the front of
the synagogue as they pray.

Services are held every day in the **synagogue.** The most important is on the morning of **Shabbat** (see pages 20–21). A service has prayers and readings from the Torah.

In the synagogue, people cover their heads to show respect. Here, the men are wearing prayer caps.

The rabbi stands on a raised platform at the front of the synagogue, facing towards Jerusalem.

A service is often led by a Jewish teacher or religious leader, called a rabbi. The rabbi may also give a talk about that day's Torah reading. He or she helps to explain what it means.

Some Jews have verses from the Torah in a small box with leather straps which they wrap around their arm during prayers.

Prayer is very important for Jews. It is a way of spending time with God. Many Jews pray three times a day — in the morning, afternoon and evening. Prayers are said in **Hebrew**.

At morning prayers, some Jews wear a prayer shawl, like a large scarf. It is called a tallit. They wrap it around their shoulders to show that God is all around them.

The prayer shawl has strings in the corners tied in a special way, which is described in the Torah.

Family times

Shabbat is the most important day of the week for Jews. It is the Jewish day of rest and prayer. It is when Jews remember how God rested after creating the universe.

Candles are lit at the start of Shabbat.

Shabbat begins on Friday evening. The mother of the family lights two candles to welcome Shabbat. Many Jews go to the **synagogue**. Afterwards, there is a special family meal at home.

The Shabbat meal often includes special bread called challah.

When a Jewish boy is 13 years old, a special ceremony is held for him in the **synagogue.** The ceremony is called Bar Mitzvah. It marks the start of the boy's adult life.

The Bar Mitzvah is when a boy becomes a full member of the Jewish community.

At her Bat Mitzvah ceremony, a girl reads from the Torah.

A Jewish girl has a similar ceremony when she is 12 years old. The ceremony is called Bat Mitzvah. In some synagogues, girls read from the Torah. In others, they give a talk.

A Jewish wedding usually takes place in a **synagogue**. During the ceremony, the couple stand under a **canopy**. It is a symbol of the home that they will share.

At a Jewish wedding, the marriage contract is read aloud and the couple are blessed by the rabbi.

A candle called a Yahrzeit is lit on the anniversary of a person's death.

When a Jew dies, there is a simple funeral service. Afterwards, there are seven days of **mourning**. Every year, a special candle is lit on the **anniversary** of the person's death.

Jewish festivals

One of the main Jewish festivals is Rosh Hashanah. It is the Jewish New Year. It falls in September or October and lasts for 10 days. It is a time for thinking back over all the good and bad things that have happened in the last year.

Apples and honey are traditionally eaten at Rosh Hashanah.

The rabbi blows a horn called a shofar at the end of Yom Kippur.

The 10th day of Rosh Hashanah is called Yom Kippur. This is when Jews ask God to forgive them for the things that they have done wrong. They promise to live better lives in the future.

Six symbolic kinds of food are eaten at Pesach.

Pesach falls in March or April. At this time, Jews remember how Moses led their **ancestors** out of Egypt more than 3,000 years ago. Families celebrate with prayers, stories, songs and a special meal.

In November or December, Jews celebrate Hanukkah. It is the festival of lights. At Hanukkah, Jews light a special candlestick with eight candles. It is called a hanukiah.

Jewish families light one candle of the hanukiah for each night of Hanukkah.

Glossary

ancestor family member who lived long ago

anniversary date remembered each year because an important event took place on that day

canopy piece of cloth hung up to make a cover or shade

Exodus departure of the Jews from Egypt led by Moses

Hebrew ancient Jewish language, now spoken in Israel

holiness the state of being holy

holy sacred, dedicated to God

Middle East part of Africa and Asia that includes Egypt, Iran, Iraq, Israel, Saudi Arabia, Syria and Turkey

mourning being very sad and missing someone who has died

Pharaoh king of ancient Egypt

presence being in a place or close by

scroll roll of parchment or paper with writing on it

Shabbat Jewish day of rest and prayer, lasting from Friday evening to Saturday evening

synagogue Jewish place of worship

Ten Commandments the first ten rules given by God to the Jewish people, teaching them how to live

Find out more

Books

A Jewish Life (Following a Faith), Cath Senker
(Franklin Watts, 2017)

Celebrating Jewish Festivals (Celebration Days), Liz Miles
(Raintree, 2016)

Jewish Festivals (A Year of Festivals), Honor Head
(Wayland, 2012)

Websites

www.bbc.co.uk/schools/religion/judaism/
Find out more about Judaism with this fact-packed website.

www.primaryhomeworkhelp.co.uk/religion/judaism.htm
Lots of information about Judaism to help you with
homework projects.

Index